George

A Memoir

Joanne Kimm

MW00912100

George: a Memoir
Copyright © 2018 by Joanne Kimm

All rights reserved. No part of this publication may be reproduced, distributed, or transmitted in any form or by any means, including photocopying, recording, or other electronic or mechanical methods, without the prior written permission of the author, except in the case of brief quotations embodied in critical reviews and certain other non-commercial uses permitted by copyright law.

Tellwell Talent
www.tellwell.ca

ISBN
978-0-2288-0523-6 (Paperback)
978-0-2288-0900-5 (eBook)

To Mitzi,
Thanks for your support,
and I hope you
enjoy George's story!
Joanne

Thank you to

The Victoria Animal Control for bringing George and our family together. Your commitment to the care of animals is greatly appreciated.

Dr. Helen Bell and the staff at Pacific Cat Clinic, who dedicate themselves every day to the health and wellbeing of our cats and kittens. We are grateful and appreciative of your caring for our George, especially at the end.

All of the animal rescue organizations. Your work is so invaluable and appreciated.

And, finally, to our beloved George...thank you for coming into our lives and bringing us so much love and joy. We will forever love you and miss you.

This is George

You might want to ask why our family wanted a cat. Don't they just lie around, eat and sleep? Are they fun or are they boring? I might answer that indeed, cats do like to lie around, eat and sleep, but they are rarely—if ever—boring! Every cat has a special personality, and every cat will bring joy and excitement into your life. Let me tell you about a special cat that did just that...his name was George.

It was December 22, 2006. Our family (me, my husband Jack, and sons Douglas and David) wanted to adopt a cat. The SPCA said they didn't have one for adoption over Christmas and suggested we visit the Victoria Animal Control; we went there the next day.

Animal Control had a big room which the cats stayed in (they called it the "cattery"). We grinned and laughed when we saw how playful and friendly the cats were with each other. Some rolled onto their backs and stretched, while others ran around and chased other cats.

After a few minutes watching the cats play, we left and walked towards another room across the way and down a hall. The room had a big window and, inside, one cat was sitting by himself. David walked over to the room and as soon as he walked by the window, the cat jumped over and started to scratch it. David walked by the window a couple of times, and each time the cat scratched at the window. We had to know why.

We asked the worker about the cat. "Why is he in that room?"

She responded, "Oh, this is the quarantine room. When we pick up animals, we separate them for a week to see if their owners claim them. If nobody comes in to claim them then we move them to either the big cat room or the big dog room."

We asked if we could meet the cat and the worker said, "I don't know. He was pretty mean when he was brought in. Let me see how he's doing today."

The worker went inside the room and saw the cat was very excited, but not mean, and she motioned for us to come inside.

We went in, and the cat walked over to us and started purring and rubbing its tail on us. I picked him up. The purring got louder.

The worker said, "I think he likes you." She took him from me and said, "He scratched the worker who picked him up as he was trying to put him in the cat cage."

I looked at the cat, then reached over and took one of his front paws. I gently squeezed it so I could see his claws, and said, "Oh, I can just snip these; they're not that bad."

The worker's mouth dropped wide in surprise. "I can't believe he let you do that," she said. "Hold on. I'm going to talk to my supervisor."

She gave me the cat and left the room. He seemed to be very happy when I held him; we all took turns petting him and he purred the whole time.

A few minutes later, she returned. "Okay, I spoke to my supervisor. She said that we will let you take him home, but because he was vicious, you can bring him back—no problem. We will totally understand if you don't want him."

We walked back to the office and, with the cat still in my arms, filled out the paperwork. I put the cat down so he could walk around. He jumped up on the desk and sniffed at the papers.

"Wow! He's curious." I laughed as I pet him. He kept purring.

"What a curious guy. Does he have a name?" I asked the worker.

She looked at the paperwork. "Nope. We just have him down as Number 1476."

"He's sure curious about what you're doing there." I laughed. "I know! Let's name him after Curious George! George for short."

Everyone laughed. "Okay. George, it is."

We finished filling out the paperwork. The worker gave us a cat kennel and said, "Remember, you can bring him back if you think he's not the right fit for your family. Considering he was pretty mean when we brought him in, we totally understand if you don't want him."

I put George into the kennel, scratched his forehead and, without any fuss, we took him home.

A few days after Christmas, we returned the kennel. At first the staff at Animal Control thought we were returning George as they couldn't see inside it, but we turned the kennel around and showed them it was empty, and they couldn't believe it! They were surprised! We told them that George picked us, and he was a great kitty so we wanted to keep him. Everyone smiled, wished us well and thanked us for adopting him.

Chapter 2

We already had two cats at home when we adopted George. One was Micki, an 18-year-old feline who'd been a part of our family for 16 years. Micki was old and sick; her kidneys weren't working that well anymore and the vet, Dr. Bell, had told us she wouldn't be around for much longer. The other cat was Tabi; she was three years old, the same age as George. Tabi was a young, playful cat, and we hoped she and George would become friends and spend time together as companions.

We brought George into the house and opened the kennel. He poked his head out, sniffed and then stepped slowly out of it. He padded around downstairs, smelling the family room, bathroom and bedroom. We didn't rush him to go upstairs where the other two cats were; we wanted him to take his time getting to know his new home. So, we just watched while he got to know his new home.

Finally, George found the stairs leading to the second floor. He walked up them, smelling each step one by one, and looked around cautiously. At the top, he walked to the left and into the master bedroom, then into the bathroom, then out and down the hall into the kitchen and living room where Micki and Tabi were lying by the fireplace.

Tabi saw George and got up. She walked over to him, stopping a few inches in front of him. They sniffed each other, then Tabi swatted George and ran away—but not too far, we saw her continue watching him from the kitchen. George walked over to Micki and smelled her. She lifted her head, stood up and stretched from the warmth of the fireplace; then she looked at George. They didn't hiss or growl at each other—they just stared.

Then, George swatted Micki on the bum. She hissed at him and ran down the hall to the bedroom while George sauntered over to the fireplace and curled up.

Tabi sat for a little while watching George, then got curious and crept over to him. She sniffed him then jumped up on top of the couch and lay down. In a few moments, they both fell asleep.

We went about our daily routine, keeping an eye on the cats to make sure George wasn't showing aggression. Sometimes cats don't like each other and will fight, so we wanted to make sure everyone was being friendly.

Over the next few months, Micki and George didn't really get along that well. Whenever we brought Micki back home from a visit with Dr. Bell, George would sniff her, swat at her and chase her into the bedroom. I guess she must have smelled bad or like the hospital; animals can sense and smell things that humans can't, so we thought George must have known she wasn't feeling well.

Then, one night Micki had a seizure in the kitchen. She was lying on the floor when her body started twitching, and she peed. After she was finished, she looked up at me. I stroked her fur gently, picked her up and took her to the washroom to clean her up. That night, she meowed a lot; we knew she was in pain.

The next day, we brought her to Dr. Bell for her last visit. Her kidneys had failed and there was nothing more we could do for her. I held Micki in my arms while Dr. Bell gave her an injection that would put her to a deep sleep, and then make her heart stop. I knew it was painless for her, but I cried anyways as I loved her very much. It was a very sad day.

When we got home, both George and Tabi walked around looking for Micki—they sensed she wasn't there. Tabi would jump up on the bed at night and walk on me, and then curl up by my head and purr. George would jump up on us when we were on the couch and lay in our laps. I think they knew I was sad. This behaviour lasted a few weeks; then, it seemed that life for them got back to normal as they settled down into their usual routine and didn't fuss about us any more.

Chapter 3

Three years after we brought George home, our family went to Disneyland. My neighbour's son offered to feed and look after the cats while we were away, and we were happy someone they knew would be taking care of them.

We had a great time at Disneyland, but the night we got home I noticed George was acting weird: he was struggling and straining every time he tried to use the litter box.

Since it was evening and Dr. Bell's office was closed, I called the pet hospital. I told them George was struggling to use the litter box and they said to bring him in as it could be life-threatening if a cat can't go to the bathroom. Panicking, we quickly put George in the cat kennel and drove over.

At the hospital, the vet examined George and told us some bad news: George had crystals in his urinary tract. We had no idea what that meant, but we soon learned that cats can develop them and that it's more common in male cats because their urinary tracts are longer than a female cat's, and the crystals can get stuck.

The vet shaved off a small bit of fur on George's front paw and hooked him up to a saline solution they could give to him intravenously (through a needle in the arm and into his veins) to, hopefully, flush the crystals out. The vet said they would need to keep George overnight and they would let us know how he was doing in the morning.

The next morning, the hospital staff called to say that George seemed to be doing better. There was a small amount of pee in the litter box they had placed in his cage; however, they felt he couldn't go home yet, so they wanted to keep him one more day. I asked if we could visit and was told yes, in fact, it would probably be good for George to see a familiar face.

We all went over to the hospital that night. The nurse brought us to the back to George's cage, and, when he saw us, he started meowing and tried to stand up. The nurse told us we could hold him, but couldn't put him down because he was still hooked up to the saline solution. He had been peeing more, and that was a good sign that the crystals were getting flushed out of his system. She reached into George's cage and pulled him out. He hissed at her, but then she placed him in my arms and he looked up and smelled my nose. He meowed and started purring. He nurse said he was happy to see me, and that he was such a different cat when I wasn't around. I told her it was because he was scared.

We held him for a long time, talking to him and petting him. He nestled into my arms and closed his eyes. But soon after, we had to put George back in his cage because the vet wanted to run more tests before letting him go home in the morning.

George meowed loudly when the nurse shut the door to his cage. He pawed the door, wanting out.

"It's okay, George," I said as I reached into the cage with my fingers, stroking his head as far as I could reach. "We'll see you in the morning."

Reluctantly, we left him and went home.

The next morning, we received a call that George was ready to come home; the fluids had been able to flush out the crystals and he was peeing normally. We were so happy!

But, two days later, we noticed he was having the same problems again, so we brought him back to the hospital. This time, the visit didn't go so well.

The doctor told us that George had crystals again, and they could try to flush them out once more but there was no guarantee they would be gone. The only other options were to put him down (like we had to do with Micki) or to do surgery to help him pee better.

We couldn't end George's life—it wasn't his fault he kept getting crystals—so, we chose the surgery.

The surgery took all day and George stayed in the hospital for an additional two days after. He wasn't happy. As soon as he was able to pee normally, eat and drink, the vet said he could go home. We were told that we would have to see our own vet to take out the stitches but, otherwise, he would be okay.

On the third day, we took George home. He wore a plastic cone around his neck to stop him from licking at his stitches. We laughed as we watched him walk around and bump into things with it! When he sauntered around the house, the cone wobbled back and forth. Even trying to eat out of the food dish proved to be difficult. We had to put the dish on a small box so it was off the floor and George could eat without the cone getting in the way. Poor George!

After a few days, we were able to take the cone off and that made him happy. He strutted around the house like he was a proud kitty! Happily, George never had issues with crystals in his urinary tract again.

Chapter 4

George seemed to get happier as the months went by. He would chase Tabi around the house playfully and she would run away or jump up on something high so he couldn't reach her. George was big and bulky whereas Tabi was very thin and light, so she could jump high and look down on him while he paced below her, looking up to see if she would jump down.

The cats loved to scratch their tall scratching post. They all loved to jump up on it and would scratch it with determination when they played together. Sometimes, all three of them would be climbing and scratching the post while chasing each other.

George was never a big jumper. A couch or bed offered little challenge, but jumping onto the window sill was a major effort; sometimes, he would miss the window and spill onto the floor. He loved to look out the window and would often scratch it so that someone would open it for him so he could feel the fresh air. He could stare outside for hours. We could only guess what he was watching; he was just happy to feel the breeze and watch the world around him.

George loved to be around people, especially Douglas and David. After dinner, when we watched TV, he would jump up on our laps or crawl up onto our chests and make himself comfortable.

It wasn't so convenient for his host, who would be trying to focus on whatever show they were watching at the time. If we wanted to get up, he would jump off, but not before digging in his claws just before he jumped down. We would often have small cuts from his sharp claws!

A cat's claws can easily scratch and draw blood; we liked to keep them short, otherwise they become little weapons. Long, sharp nails would often hurt us when George swatted us during playtime. Take it from me: a bloody scratch is no fun!

We could all tell when it was time to cut George's claws. Lying in bed, in the quiet of night, we would hear *tick tick tick* as he walked across the floor. That's when we knew it was time to cut his nails.

I would often snip George's claws with nail clippers. And while that may sound easy—it wasn't.

The cats seemed to know when I brought out the nail clippers; they would try and run away, which made it challenging to catch them. Tabi would jump on something high and we had to wait for her to come down, but poor George! Being a bit bigger and bulkier in weight, he was always the first one we caught. He fussed when Jack held him and I tried to quickly cut his nails, while at the same time trying not to get nipped at or scratched. Luckily, the nails didn't grow too long, but it sure made nail-cutting day interesting!

Chapter 5

In February 2013, I started work in a new office. I really liked it, and it was close to home. I was working for about six months when I found out some really interesting news.

One of my co-workers had found a kitten; she'd found it that morning in a pipe that surrounded the office building, and someone had managed to pull it out. A few more kittens were also found in the pipe and they, too, had been pulled out and brought to the animal rescue—poor things! The one my co-worker had found, however, was in a box under her desk.

When I went downstairs to look at the kitten, my co-worker told me to be very careful because it was scared.

I opened the box slowly and looked inside. Down at the bottom was a black ball of fluff: a very scared and shaky kitten. It looked up at me and meowed softly. I slowly put my hand down and pet it lightly. I guessed that it couldn't be more than eight weeks old.

I closed the box and told my co-worker that I wanted to take the kitten home; she said I could take it if I brought it to the vet to be checked out.

I called home and told Jack I would like to have the cat. He said he wasn't sure, as George might hurt it. I told him we could lock up the kitten for a few days, and then slowly let it get used to the other cats. Jack agreed to this and came over to the office to pick me up.

When we got to Dr. Bell's office, everyone was surprised to see the big box we brought with us. We were led to the back room where it was quieter.

Dr. Bell was away, so another vet came in along with two assistants. The vet snapped on some gloves, opened the box, and reached inside. We heard a loud *hiss*, then a spitting sound, and then the vet quickly pulled out her hand. We all gasped at what we saw: her glove had been shredded by the kitten!

She peeled off the glove, checked her hands for cuts (which had none, thankfully), put on another glove and reached inside the box again. This time, she was quick to pull out the black ball of hissing, spitting fluff. It was the first time I saw my kitten—she was scared!

The vet handed her to me and I cuddled her close to my chest, murmuring and speaking quietly, while gently stroking her. She relaxed a little bit. The vet then asked for the kitten to be put on the table for examination and the assistants helped me put the kitten down (as she was trying to hide under my hair) and took over.

They looked over her body, listened to her heart and cleaned her fur. The kitten squirmed and hissed, but when the assistants put her back in my arms, she snuggled into me once again. After the check-up, the assistants gave us a small carry-box so we could put her inside and take her home.

When we got home, we brought the kitten into our bedroom and shut the door. We opened the box and watched as she slowly crept out. We sat on the floor nearby so she wouldn't be scared and she wobbled over to us, sniffed us and then ran under the bed where she stayed for the rest of the night. We brought some food, water and a small litter box for her and put them in the bathroom.

The next day, we noticed she had used the litter box and eaten some food, so we were happy. The next step was to introduce her to the other two cats.

We waited a few days before letting George or Tabi into the bedroom. George didn't understand why we had the bedroom door shut, so he'd been scratching it often to get in.

But, on the third day (and once the kitten was feeling safe) we let him in.

I was holding the kitten, and Jack held George; we brought the two cats close together to let them smell each other and because we didn't know if George would try to beat up the kitten. They sniffed each other, then the kitten reached over and swatted George on the nose and hissed. She jumped out of my hands and skittered under the bed. George just watched her. Jack put him down and we both stayed in the room to make sure the cats would be okay. The kitten came out from under the bed and slowly approached George. He just stared at her again and walked away.

Pretty soon, the kitten got used to George, so we introduced her to Tabi. Again, the kitten hissed and ran away, but later came out and sniffed Tabi.

A few days after that, we were able to open the bedroom door all the time and let the kitten explore the house. She was so small though, and she liked to crawl into drawers and small places; we never knew where she was hiding and would nervously search all over the house whenever she disappeared. One time, she crawled up the back of my bedside table and it took us two hours to find her inside the top drawer!

At work, people were happy I had taken the kitten home. They would often ask how the kitten was doing and wondered what name I would call her. A lot of my co-workers sent me suggestions; some people suggested I call her "Stormy" or "Piper," but in the end I thought of "Tia"—it just seemed to suit her.

And so, Tia it was...

Chapter 6

George, Tabi and Tia got along well. They ate together, sometimes lie around the house all together, and played with each other. George would chase Tabi, Tia would chase George, and Tabi would run away. Things seemed to be pretty good until 2015.

The house we lived in at that time had a huge backyard, and we put up a badminton net that summer. That meant we were outside a lot, running around in the grass.

One day, I noticed George was scratching a lot. He'd also started licking himself so much that some of his fur was being pulled out and we noticed a lot of bald patches on him. I picked

him up and was about to pet him when I saw this tiny black bug crawling on him—George had a flea! I quickly put him on the floor and called Dr. Bell's office. I was surprised because the cats didn't go outside, and I was wondering where the fleas had come from. We figured that the fleas were probably outside in the lawn and had come inside on one of the boys after playing badminton.

Dr. Bell treated each of the cats, but, because George had been licking himself so much and his fur was coming out, they had to put on a cone around his neck to stop him from licking himself bald. Yet another cone! Poor George!

George only had to wear the cone for about a week, until his skin was feeling better. But he certainly did not like wearing it! We laughed as he tried walking around the house, bumping into walls and furniture. I think his ego took a big hit! Even though we felt bad for him, it was a funny sight to watch.

Chapter 7

George loved to be around people or the other cats. Most days, he would sit on the couch, but he also loved to lay on the cushions. Sometimes, he would dive underneath the bedding when we were making the bed. He would peek out underneath his little "fortress" and swat us when we tried to get him out. A string or light would soon entice him to come out to play, and then we could quickly finish making the bed.

When friends would come over to play cards, George would often jump up on the bench next to me and look at what was going on. He sometimes pawed at the cards making it look like he was in the game. He was certainly very curious!

George liked Christmastime, too. He especially enjoyed sleeping underneath the Christmas tree or sitting by it; though, he never tried to climb it, unlike Tia. Tia would jump into the Christmas tree and climb up to the top, shaking it so much that we worried she might topple it over! George, on the other hand, would find a spot close by, sit and watch us try frantically to get Tia out of the tree. We found the best way to get her out of the tree was to shake the treat container. She would

then squirm down, shaking the tree even more, to get a treat. The only problem was that all the cats expected treats!

For playtime, George and Tia would play in their cathouse, which sat on the top of the scratch post. It was funny to watch George swat frantically at Tia as she sat on the top of the house and teased him! Cats sure are smart! They like to wait for the perfect moment to pounce!

The Last Chapter

Over the last few years, George got sicker. We noticed his fur had started to become thinner and he was spending more time by himself.

We took him to Dr. Bell and she took blood and pee samples to test as well as some X-rays. We discovered that George had cancer in the lining of his stomach, which meant it wasn't able to absorb the nutrients in his food, so he wasn't able to stay healthy. Dr. Bell put him on a few medications and, over the span of a few months, he seemed to get better. His fur grew in thicker, he ate and drank more, and became more playful with Tabi and Tia.

One of the medications was a cancer pill, which was toxic (dangerous to touch and could not be broken up and put in food). It had to be given to George in his mouth by hand and Jack would have to bring George into Dr. Bell's office every third week of the month so the staff at the clinic could give it to him; we wanted to make sure he took it properly. Dr. Bell told us that because the cancer would only get worse, George would probably only be with us for two more years; medication would help him to be more comfortable, but we should prepare ourselves for when he got sick again. It was upsetting to hear this news, but we understood there was no cure for him.

After a year on the medication, Dr. Bell ran some tests which showed George was improving, so his cancer medication was cut back a little bit. We were happy because we could see he was getting back to his usual, playful self again. But, in early 2018, we noticed George wasn't eating or drinking as much, spent most of his time sleeping and moved to other parts of the living room to be by himself. We remembered how Dr. Bell had told us he would only be with us for about two more years, but only a year had passed and it was becoming clear he would not make it to the two-year mark. My heart broke thinking he was suffering.

The day before George died, on February 20, 2018, he walked away from us and sat at the landing on the top of the stairs. He stayed there for the whole evening.

The next morning, he was still there. I came home from work at lunchtime and he was still sitting in the same spot. I put a bowl of water by him, but he refused to drink. Before I went back to work, I pet him and put my head on his tummy. I heard a little rumbling, but I wasn't sure if he was trying to purr or whether his heart wasn't working properly. I scratched him gently on the head and he lifted his head up higher for me to scratch his ears.

I went back to work, but in my heart I knew he wasn't going to make it. He was really sick. I remembered reading how animals will go somewhere to be alone when they are very sick or dying, and I knew George was telling us he was sick. He didn't hide because he still wanted to be close to us, but at the same time, he was trying to be by himself.

I knew I had to make a very tough phone call. I called Dr. Bell's office and told them what was happening. The staff made an appointment for us to bring George in—it would be his last visit.

I called home to let David and Jack know what was going on and told them George would not be coming home after visit with Dr. Bell. We talked about how sick George was and how it wasn't fair to George to make him suffer.

When I got home from work, I picked George up and held him close. He felt so light. He purred and snuggled in closer. We all pet him and spoke our last goodbyes.

Then Jack and I put him into the cat carrier and left; David stayed home.

George meowed loudly on the way to Dr. Bell's office. He didn't normally meow for the ride, so we knew he was upset or hurting.

When we got to the Dr. Bell's office, the assistant took us into a private room, and when we were inside, we took George out of the cat carrier and put him on the floor for the assistant to look him over. He could barely walk and his legs gave out on him. I picked him up and cradled him closely to my chest. The assistant told us how sorry she was to see how sick George was, got up, and left to get the doctor.

I sat down on the chair. George lay in my arms and started to purr.

The assistant came back in to the room with another vet. She was working in the office that day due to Dr. Bell being away.

She smiled sadly at us and told us how sorry she as to see us under these circumstances, then examined George. She could see he wasn't doing well. The assistant sat next to me as the vet explained what she would be doing for George.

George would be given medication to make him sleep. George, we were told, would feel nothing. After he was in a deep, deep sleep, the vet would then give him a dose of the drug that would make his heart stop.

I cried a lot and the assistant gave me a big bunch of Kleenex so I could wipe my eyes. George kept purring while lying in my arms.

The vet and the assistant left the room to let the medication take effect. While we were alone with George, Jack and I talked softly to him. I could feel his body get heavier as he fell into a deep sleep. I had to adjust him in my arms so that he wouldn't slide out and fall.

George kept purring. I kept crying.

After about five or six minutes, the vet and the assistant came back into the room. The vet listened to George's heart and confirmed he was in a very deep sleep. Then they gave him the final dose of medication, and, in a few moments, George stopped purring. He was dead.

The vet took out her stethoscope and listened to his heart. She told me that there was no more heartbeat. I cried loudly and cradled him closer.

The assistant asked if she could take him, but I said, "No." I wanted to hold him as long as I could, because I wasn't ready to say goodbye to him yet. I asked the assistant what would happen to George and she said that he would be cremated, but, if we wanted, the person who did the cremation would shave off some of his hair for us and put it in a card so that we would have a memento of him (a remembrance card). I said that I would like that very much.

I asked if I could bring George to the back room and lay him out on the table so I could say goodbye, and the vet said that would be okay. I got up and carried him into the back room. The assistant put a towel on the table and I lay George down on it; he looked so peaceful.

"He looks like he's just sleeping," I said. I pet him. His fur was soft to the touch, and I stroked his body. I lifted up one of his back legs and laughed, "Remember how he was always needing his back claws cut and he hated it when I tried? They don't look too bad, actually."

I put the leg back down and pet him again.

One of the other office assistants came into the back room. She was one of the staff that had helped give George his cancer medication.

"I'm so sorry about George," she said, stroking him. "He was a great kitty. We really loved him."

The vet, the staff, Jack and I stayed for almost another hour talking about George. I told some funny stories about him while continuing to pet him.

Then, it was time to leave. I took a picture of him on the table so I would have one last memory. He looked like he was just stretched out and sleeping, looking comfortable.

I cried all the way home.

At home, Tabi and Tia walked around, smelling the cat cage. I think they knew George wouldn't be coming back.

After a few days, we noticed Tabi was following us around and jumping up on the chair next to us. I don't know if she understood we were upset about George, but she acted very differently.

A few weeks later, Tabi still followed us around the house, played with Tia more and seemed more energetic. Tia, on the other hand, didn't change her behaviour at all; she still acted like she was the boss but spent more time playing with Tabi.

While we know George is not suffering any more and life must go on, his loss has deeply cut into our hearts. Sometimes I cry when I look at his pictures, and I often talk about him, laughing at the funny things he did and remembering how much he loved to be around us especially when we played cards! I also look at the remembrance card we received after his death, and remember the *tick tick tick* of his claws on the floor. It puts a smile on my face because I'll never forget that sound.

And so, you might ask: why would anyone want a cat? Because they give us so much joy in our hearts and make our lives more meaningful. Sure, they like to live simply—lying around, sleeping and eating, but, they also love us, too, and show it in many different ways even if it's when they rub up against our legs or just lie on our chest when we're trying to watch TV!

George was a much-loved member of our family and we are so very, very grateful for the fate that brought us together. While we will always miss him, we also have big smiles in our hearts when we remember all the funny and heartfelt times we shared. And, I still have the scars on my arms from him-those will never go away. They will always be a constant reminder of him and how he hated getting his nailed clipped!

George hiding amongst some
packing boxes

Dinnertime for Tia,
Tabi and George

Tia and Tabi

George playing with the
"wobbly" – treats inside!

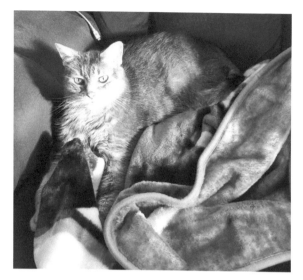

Christmas 2017 – George enjoying
my new blanket!

George looking out the window
at Christmastime

George and Tia enjoying the
view out the window

George sitting on the bench,
saying hello to me after I've
come home from work

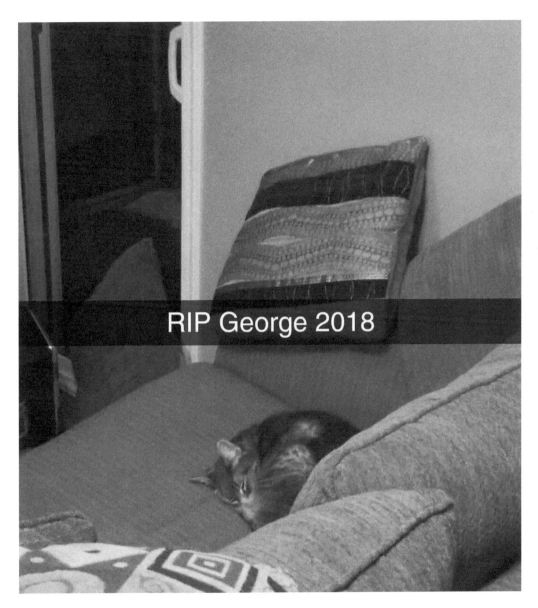

RIP George 2018

December 23, 2006 - February 21, 2018

CPSIA information can be obtained
at www.ICGtesting.com
Printed in the USA
BVHW022006110319
542354BV00004B/15/P

9780228805236